THE KEY TO LANDING A JOB   THE INTERVIEW

THE KEY TO LANDING A JOB – THE INTERVIEW

Interview Secrets That Employers And Headhunters
Don't Want You To Know.

By Professor Michael Manahan, MBA

To all of those wonderful students who have taken my classes over the years, who put up with me as a professor, and from whom I learned so much.

Are you a Zebra? What do zebras have to do with getting a job? Nothing and everything. Ever wonder why do we ride horses and not zebras? The reason is that zebras do not get along with people. Zebras don't even get along that well with the other zebras. At some point in the interview, the interviewer is going to try to find out if you are a zebra. Do you get along well with people?

CA. MAY 2020 | MICHAEL S. MANAHAN

CONTENTS

PREFACE

One day sometime in 2019 a student of mine (I'll call her Debra) said she was going on a job interview, and she asked me, as one of her professors, if I could give her some ideas that might help her do a better job during the interview, which would help her get the job. I said, of course. Debra was one of my accounting students, she did well in class, and she was serious about her education. I was happy to help.

Over the next couple of days, I thought about interview techniques, and then later in the week, I met with Debra. Our conversation lasted about an hour and a half while I coached Debra on ideas and strategies I thought would help her ace the interview and get the job. Debra got the job, and one thing she mentioned to me was that she knew nothing about interviews and that what I had told her made the difference. She then suggested that I write down all the ideas I had given her to share with her fellow students. That was the genesis for this book.

As my manuscript grew, I kept conducting research on the Internet on various websites that have articles, videos, and pointers on how to do well in interviews. I wanted to find out if there were any breakthroughs, revelations, or fabulous ideas that I hadn't thought of. There is a lot of excellent information you can find on the Internet about improving your interview skills. Further, in addition to this book, I would encourage you to check out a few of these websites. However, I found that most websites did not have the detail that I thought was necessary to really understand good interview techniques (particularly for those people who haven't done a lot of interviews). Further, I thought many of them lacked good examples that could provide a template for someone trying to improve their interview skills. Finally, I think my book has some ideas that you simply won't find on the major job interview websites (at least I couldn't find them). Therefore, I believe what I have written adds to the body of work that is already available.

I also point out that this book does not cover everything. I do mention video interviews, which are becoming increasingly important. You can use many of the techniques in this book for video interviews, but if you think you will be doing a lot of video interviews, you may want to do some additional research.

Also, I do not cover such things as group interviews and out of the office interviews (such as at restaurants). Again, many of the techniques and strategies discussed in this book can help with those types of interviews, but if you think you may be doing a lot of those interviews, you will want to do additional research.

There is another reason that I wrote this book. As a professor teaching finance and accounting, I know what my students learn in the classroom will help them once they have a job. But as a consultant and before that as an employee, I also recognize that just having the technical toolkit to do the job is not enough. More than once in my career, I went for interviews for jobs where I was not the one hired, only to find out months later that the person who had been hired didn't work out. The company hired the wrong person. The more interviews I went on, the more I came to realize hiring someone is not like accounting. The people who get hired may be good at the job, but chances are they are great at interviews. And the people who get the best jobs are just that much better at interviews.

INTRODUCTION

During my forty-plus years of experience as a member of management or as a consultant, I hired or was part of the team that hired hundreds of employees. Given that I hired hundreds of employees, I estimate that I interviewed over the course of forty years more than 1,000 candidates. As someone doing the hiring, I can assure you that the one thing that has the most impact on a candidate getting hired is the interview.

A good resume is needed. That will get you in the door. Some companies may administer skill tests (such as Excel) or psychological tests (such as Meyers Briggs). Some companies will do background checks, and others will do reference checks. However, the most important assessment of you as a candidate occurs during the interview. In the interview, you will shine, or you will be outperformed by others. Typically, in interviews, one or two candidates do much better than the rest of the candidates. This statistic is not just true for junior or entry-level jobs but also for senior-level and executive positions. I was part of the committees to hire accounting professors and an assistant dean for the School of Business at California State University Dominguez Hills, and I was amazed at how poorly these educated, intelligent candidates with Doctoral Degrees performed during interviews. Many of the interviewees lacked even the basics of good inter-

1

view techniques.

When I started teaching, one of the first classes I taught was Business Communications. Most business communications courses include segments on seeking employment, creating resumes, and going to interviews. The information in the textbooks that I read contained excellent recommendations (and if you have not read any such textbooks, you should), but I always found something missing from those recommendations. That inspired me to write down some of the things that I observed during my career that made me think well of a candidate and put that candidate near or at the top of the list of the candidates I wanted to hire. In this guidebook, you may find information that you already know, so hopefully, it will be a good reminder for you about successful interviews. If some of the ideas and tactics are unknown to you, then learn them and use them to your advantage during the job interview.

Finally, a good interview is not just about getting the job. An interview is a two-way street. A good interview gives you the opportunity of assessing a prospective employer and the people you will be working with at that prospective employer. The company wants to make sure the candidate it hires is the best fit for that organization, and you want to make sure that the company is the best fit for you. Using some of the ideas and suggestions in this guidebook will not only increase the likelihood of you getting the job offer but will also give you better information in which to assess whether the company is someplace you really want to work.

DON'T BE LATE

I live in the greater Los Angeles area, and due to our gridlocked freeways, it seems a lot of people I meet for business meetings are late. Some people I know are just chronically late. Maybe you can be that way and still do business, but if you are trying to get a job, being late leaves an awful impression. I cannot recall ever hiring someone who was late for the interview.

Being just on time is only a little better than being late. Latecomers need to apologize, which means those candidates start off on the wrong foot, but those who arrive just on time are often rushed and stressed from battling traffic, finding parking, and making sure they have arrived at the correct location. If the weather is warm, you could also be dripping with sweat, which just doesn't look right. Latecomers or just-in-time candidates don't have a few extra minutes for a final check in the mirror or to relax prior to the interview.

My recommendation? Plan to be an hour early to an interview. Find the location, find the parking, then drive a couple of blocks down the street and find a coffee shop or restaurant. Spend the time prior to the interview, preparing for the interview, reviewing the things I will discuss in the following sections, and destressing, so that when you walk in the front door of the office building, you are relaxed and composed. Right off the bat, you are ahead of the curve because most other candidates will arrive just on time, or late.

You also want to make sure you don't arrive too early. Walking in the door five minutes early is okay. Any more than that and you could be too early. Sitting in a lobby waiting for half an hour while people walk in and out staring at you could be unnerving, and not all employers are well set up to host people they are not ready to see.

APPEARANCE COUNTS

I t's just a simple fact that people are attracted to things that look good. A clean polished car looks better than one covered in dirt and dust. That same appeal works with people. Having interviewed over 1,000 candidates, I can tell you many candidates do not dress and groom appropriately, and that could cost you the interview. What does it mean to dress and groom appropriately? To me, it means clothes that are clean, clothes that fit properly, and clothes that conform to business attire. I may be a little old school, but for men, that means a suit and tie with hard-soled shoes that are nicely polished. I don't care if everyone in the company you are interviewing with is dressed in T-shirts and board shorts – you should wear a suit and tie, or for ladies, an appropriately conservative business outfit. Men seem to have this problem more than women, but I could not count the times I have interviewed a man whose suit fits so poorly I wasn't even sure if it was that person's suit. Spend the money to get clothes that fit your body. For women, footwear can be important. A colleague relates the story of a candidate that wore high heels, and as a result, the candidate was not allowed into the factory due to safety issues.

Of course, you should do your research. For some companies who have a very casual dress code, the interviewers would be fine with you showing up casual. But showing up casual should be the result of your research, not a guess on your part. As an example, I have been told that if you get interviewed by Trader Joe's wearing a Hawaiian shirt to the interview is acceptable because staff members at Trader Joe's wear Hawaiian shirts.

Grooming is important too. For men, that means combed hair and a shaved face unless you have a nicely trimmed beard. Don't bother wearing cologne. These days when everyone seems to be allergic to something, you will find strong cologne could be a problem. For women, it means conservative use of makeup and again, don't bother with the perfume. You're going to an interview, not a Vegas night club.

For those of you who are into body art (AKA tattoos), the rule is simple. Do your best to hide them.

Now there are exceptions to the rule, and if possible, when you are scheduling an interview, you should attempt to find out if there are any special requirements in dressing for the interview. As an example, if the interview will include a plant tour, and the plant is a dirty, messy industrial plant, you may need to wear clothes that are appropriate for the environment, like jeans and work boots. If in doubt, overdress rather than underdress.

DON'T FORGET THE SUPPORT STAFF

When I say support staff, I am talking about the people you meet when you arrive for an interview. In many companies, you will meet a receptionist, coordinator, junior HR person, or administrative assistant first. That person may have you complete certain forms, may escort you to the conference or waiting room, may show you where the bathroom is, and may offer you coffee and water. You may think these people are unimportant. If you do, you're wrong. Do everything you can to build rapport and make a good impression with these people. I have seen presidents and CEOs interviewing for major executive positions who, after an interview, walked out to the reception desk and asked the receptionist, "Well, what did you think of him?" When the final decision comes down to two or three candidates, other people who had contact with the candidates may be asked for their opinion, even though they may not have spent much time with the candidate.

My recommendation is that you do everything you can to try to connect with receptionists, administrative assistants, and even current employees of the company you might meet in the break room. Ask them their name. Ask them what they do for the company. Ask them how they like the company. Tell them how excited you are and how much you like the company. Show these people as much deference and respect as if they were the presi-

7

dent of the company. Remember, in any company, you are going to have arrogant managers, salespersons, and professionals who think they are above the support staff. The very fact that you treat people who may be on the low end of the organization chart with the respect they deserve could get you a good word from those people to the interviewer. And if nothing else, it's a good habit to develop and the right thing to do.

A friend of mine who is a recruiter started his career working at the front desk of his employer. He tells the story of the human resources manager coming out to the front counter to ask about candidates' manners and politeness and about his overall impression of candidates. Remember, everyone is judging you, and in some organizations, the opinions of the support staff really count.

PHONE AND VIDEO INTERVIEWS

In this guidebook, I discuss the "interview" as if the first time you will meet with the interviewer is in a face to face meeting. That may be the case. However, today many companies, particularly larger employers, conduct phone interviews and video interviews in advance of a face to face meeting. The guidelines for phone interviews and video interviews are the same as for face to face interviews, excepting that certain recommendation I will make in this guidebook may be a little more challenging to orchestrate on the phone or on a video conference, simply because you don't have the opportunity to visually see the environment in which the interview is taking place, and the interviewer does not have the ability to see what you are doing or what you may have prepared for the interview. Preparation is the key. The more you are prepared for phone interviews and video interviews (using the guidelines in this book), the better you will do.

In a phone interview, the interviewer obviously cannot see you. Therefore, all the interviewer has to go on is your voice. Thus, in phone interviews, it is extremely important to speak clearly and to be in a place where there is no background noise. If you are using your cell phone, make sure you are in a location that has good cell phone service. Don't use your speakerphone or headset as those can cause feedback and other unwanted sound effects. When we speak, our speech is often accompanied by facial expressions and hand gestures. Again, the interviewer cannot see any of those on a phone interview, so make an extra effort to use an expression in your voice to convey interest and enthusiasm. I recommend recording yourself answering a few common interview questions to see what you sound like. Maybe even ask a friend or relative to listen to those recordings. Listen to the radio and note how radio hosts use their voices to express anger, frustration, enthusiasm, excitement, and interest. Try adopting some of these voice techniques. How you sound over the phone could be the difference between getting a face-to-face interview, or being passed over for the next candidate.

For video interviews, you also need to make sure you are dressed appropriately (as for face-to-face interviews). Check your distance from the camera on your laptop. You don't want to be too close, and you don't want to be too far away. For video interviews, it is very important that you look into the camera. In a face-to-face interview, you want to have eye contact, but in a video, it is important to pretend you have eye contact. It is very disconcerting to interview someone by video if that person is staring at the ceiling or looking at the floor. Also, make sure you choose a good background. Either a blank wall, or a conservative backdrop is best. Even better if you can somehow get a bookcase full of books into the picture (with a selection of business books on it). If you have bizarre artwork, rap posters, or some other odd paraphernalia in the room, make sure it's not in the picture.

BREAK DOWN
THE WALLS

The very first thing you need to do when you walk into the interview room is to "break down the walls" (I am assuming here that your first interview is a face to face interview, but if your first interview is a phone or video interview, the same rules apply). What do I mean by that? The interviewer is suspicious about the candidate. The interviewer knows little about the candidate other than what is on the resume, and in many cases, the interviewer has not read the resume in detail because an assistant or someone in human resources set up the interview. So, the interviewer has no connection to the candidate and, like any stranger, is more inclined to view the candidate and the candidate's answers negatively. Interviewers will be skeptical. They want to see the fit between the person and the job, and the interviewer also needs to see "personality."

Your job is to as quickly as possible, break down the walls by developing rapport with the interviewer. That means showing in some way that you have common ground or common interests, and at the very least, that you have some interest in the interviewer as a person, as opposed to just being interested in the interviewer because he/she is the boss.

Why do you want to develop rapport? Simple. If you ever read any books about dealing with people from Dale Carnegie's How to Win Friends and Influence People published in 1936 to the hundreds of books on dating and relationships you can buy on Amazon, you will find a common theme. That common theme is you need to build rapport with the other person. When you build rapport with another person, that person is more trusting of you, is more likely to overlook your flaws, and starts to think of you as part of that person's community or tribe. I use community and tribe in a very broad sense because today, we are all members of groups with similar identities, at least with respect to certain ideals, activities, interests, and beliefs. As an example, if I am an avid golfer, and I meet someone who is either an avid golfer, or who wants to be, I can very quickly develop rapport. We have something to talk about—we have something in common. We are both members of the community or tribe of golfers.

How do you develop rapport? It is not that difficult, but you must do a little work, and you may have to be creative. Whenever you accept an invitation for a job interview, you should always find out who will be interviewing you. Often interviews are scheduled by an administrative assistant or someone from the human resources department. Some companies may not volunteer the name of the interviewer, and if the person scheduling the interview does not, you need to ask. Once you have the name of the person, do some research. You can look at a company's website, search Facebook, search LinkedIn.com, or just do a Google search to find that person. Once you have found the person, find out something about that person that you can use to start a conversation. If you do find the interviewer on Facebook or LinkedIn, don't try to connect with that person online. You don't have a business relationship with that person yet – you are just doing your research. There is no need to hide the fact that you have done some research on the interviewer. Such research will show to the interviewer that you have initiative.

As an example, I Googled my name. The third search item was my name on a website called RateYourProfessor.com. I've heard of this website but never actually checked it out. I did now and found out that some students didn't like me very much. Well, that is a conversation starter. If I were going to interview you, a good question for you to ask me to break the ice would be: "I was looking to see what I could find out about you online. I came across this website Rate Your Professor and noted that you have mixed reviews. I was thinking about teaching someday, and I wonder how many students really use this site?" Now you've got my attention because you have brought up something that I am passionate about – teaching. I could talk about it for hours. And the fact that you have an interest in teaching gives us something in common (BY THE WAY, even if you don't ever plan to teach it is okay to tell someone you have an interest in his or her hobby, sport's team, charity, or activity the person involves themselves with).

What if you cannot get the name of the person who will be conducting the interview in advance? If you can't get a name, at least get a title. Sometimes companies list their managers and executives on their websites, so if you know you are meeting with the Controller, you can probably find his name on the company's website. You could also check for his name on LinkedIn. Some companies even have LinkedIn company pages that list employees and executives.

However, there are instances where, despite your best efforts, you just cannot come up with a name. Sometimes that happens, and this situation is where you need to be a little creative. If you can't find out about the person, find out something about the company. Look at the company's website. (Of course, you should be looking at the company's website anyway, and we will discuss that further later on). Do a Google search on the company's name. Trader Joe's is a big employer. I Googled Trader Joe's and the fifth item in the search results was an article in Business Insider titled "What to Buy and What Not to Buy at Trader Joe's." I read the article, and it says that you should skip buying vegetables at Trader Joe's because the vegetables are often past their prime and go bad quickly. Now I have something to talk about. If I had an interview with Trader Joe's, I could start off the interview by asking the question, "Mr. Jones, it's a pleasure to meet you, and I'm dying to ask you a question. I read this article in Business Insider that recommends not buying vegetables at Trader Joe's because those vegetables are past their prime. I have bought vegetables at Trader Joe's many times and never had a problem. How do you fight negative articles like this one?"

Okay. So now you've done a few things that will help you get the job. First, you've asked a question to get the interviewer talking, and that will help build rapport. Second, you mentioned you've bought vegetables at Trader Joe's so now you are part of the Trader Joe's community (by the way, even if you only went to Trader Joe's once in your life, you don't need to provide all of the details – the fact that you did shop at Trader Joe's makes you part of the community). Third, you have impressed the interviewer because chances are you are the only candidate who bothered to go online and read a bit of information about the company. With this one "start the interview" question, you have leaped well ahead of the other candidates who will be interviewing for the job.

If you have the opportunity to visit the company's place of business, you should do so. It's a great way to pick up information on the company's culture, its employees, and its products or operations. All this information can be used as conversation starters.

Whether or not you get the name of the interviewer, and regardless of the advance research you have done, be prepared to build rapport spontaneously based upon the information you observe when you arrive for the interview. To give you an example, years ago, before the Internet, Google searches, and LinkedIn, I went for an interview for an accounting position. I arrived at the company's office, and I was escorted into the office of the CFO of the company. I quickly noticed that his walls were covered with pictures of sailboats, and one of the pictures looked like him in a racing type sailboat. The first thing I said was, "Wow! You must be an avid sailor. I want to take sailing lessons. Any recommendations?" With that opening question, my interviewer spent the next twenty minutes talking about his boat, how he had raced in some famous sailboat race, and his yacht club. Of course, I kept asking more questions, and he kept talking. I think I was in the interview for about 45 minutes, but he must have talked for 30 of those 45 minutes and mostly about sailing. I remember at the end of the interview when he shook my hand, he said, "Great interview. You're just the type of person we're looking for." How was he able to determine that? He wasn't. But we had built a rapport over sailing.

The key is to be observant. Look at the pictures and para-phernalia in the interviewer's office. If there are golf pictures, he is probably a golfer. If there are pictures of hockey teams, he is probably a hockey fan. If there are pictures of children, he is probably a father, or grandfather. Everything you see is an opportunity for you to ask a question to get the interviewer talking about something he is passionate about. And once the interviewer is talking about something he or she is passionate about, you are building rapport, particularly if you are also passionate about the same thing, or at least seem seriously interested. Remember, even if you are not passionate about it, you can be interested. As an example, let's say the person has ski pictures in his office, but you are not a skier and don't know much about it. You can say something like, "Wow! You must be a good skier. I haven't skied, but it's something I've wanted to try for years. What's the best way to get into skiing?"

Many times, interviews will be conducted in conference rooms, so a rapport building question taken from the office environment might be difficult. That's when you need to pull the rapport building question from your previous research.

Let me re-emphasize how important it is that you start the interview with a rapport building question. That question and your conversation about that question will set a positive tone for the rest of the interview. The interviewer will be more relaxed and will judge you more leniently than he or she might otherwise judge you.

IT'S A CONVERSATION

I have conducted hundreds of interviews where I asked a list of questions, and the candidate answers each of the questions, and when I have run out of questions, I ask the candidate, "Do you have any questions?" BY THE WAY, you may get this same question, and I will discuss later how to answer that question. But if you make the interview into a conversation, you may never get asked this question.

What am I talking about? Let me give you an example. Interviewers want to know how well you get along with other people. Companies don't want troublemakers. So, you may get a question like this: "Tell me about a time you had an issue with a co-worker and how you handled that issue." I will discuss later how to answer this question too, but in answering this question, make sure you ask a question back.

What do I mean? You could start off by not answering the question, and instead asking, "Do you find that co-workers not getting along is a problem in your company?" The interviewer will answer yes or no but may also go on to relate an experience the company is now facing or faced in the past. Now you have turned the interview into a conversation. If the interviewer just answers "Yes," then you can ask the follow-up question, "I'd like to know more about that?" If the interviewer says no, then you can respond by saying something like, "That's good to know. I wouldn't want to work for a company where the employees don't get along." At this point, you may never even have to answer the initial question (if you do answer the question, I will discuss later how you should respond). It is entirely likely that the interviewer will just go on to the next question on his or her list.

You do need to be careful using this tactic. Some interviewers may think you are avoiding the question. However, in my experience, the technique works, and you can always answer the question after you have asked your probing question in response.

Keep using this tactic throughout the interview, and the interview will become more of a conversation. Instead of the interview being an interrogation by the interviewer of the candidate, it now becomes more of a conversation between an employer and a prospective employee, both trying to determine if this is a good fit.

Let me give you one more example, so you've got this down pat. Another favorite question of interviewers is, "Tell me about your weaknesses." Again, I will discuss later how to answer many of the "favorite" interview questions. But for right now, focus on not answering the question, but asking a question back. To this question, you might ask back, "From that question, it sounds like maybe you've had some people in this position that didn't perform too well. What do you think were the weaknesses of the people who've held this position in the past?" My experience says that very few interviewers will pass up the opportunity to tell you what weaknesses the previous employees had. The interviewer might say something like, "Well, the person you're replacing was extremely accurate and made very few mistakes, but at times we get super busy, and when we did, that person seemed to get overwhelmed." Now you have an opportunity to demonstrate that you work well under pressure and can hopefully use one of your demonstrations (I will explain later about demonstrations) to prove the point.

If you adopt this technique effectively, the interview will really be more like a conversation between two equal businesspeople - the kind of conversation you might have over a cup of coffee or a cocktail. The interviewer may never get to the "Now do you have any questions for me?" question because you have asked so many good questions during the interview.

Something else that is related to the conversational style is what I call the clarifying question. I often see candidates who are so anxious to answer a question that they just start talking, and I quickly realize the candidate has misunderstood the question. That is embarrassing for both the candidate and the interviewer. Make sure you really understand the question being asked, and if you are not sure, just as you would do in any conversation, ask the interviewer to restate or rephrase the question. You could also state back to the interviewer what you think the question is, just to be sure.

DO YOU HAVE ANY QUESTIONS FOR ME?

E ven if you have followed my advice so far and have asked a number of great "questions back" in response to questions you may have been asked, the interviewer may still finish off the interview by asking you, "Do you have any questions for me?" Here is how you should answer that question.

First, DO NOT ask about pay, hours, benefits, vacation, or anything that has to do with your compensation and employment package. My colleague Dr. Norman calls these "me, me, me" questions. All such discussions should be left until the company makes you an offer. Now, the interviewer may ask you questions about compensation, and I will show you how to answer those questions a little later.

In response to "Do you have any questions for me?" you should have at least five questions prepared (and it would be even better if it were ten questions). These questions could be generic (a question you could use in any interview), or these questions could be specific (a question that only applies to this company). I suggest you have some of each.

These questions should be open-ended. An open-ended question is a question for which "yes" or "no" is not an appropriate response. So, if one of your questions was about social media, you would not want to ask, "Do you use social media in your marketing activities?" The answer to that question is obviously yes or no. However, you can rephrase this question to make it open-ended. Instead ask, "Can you explain the role that social media plays in your overall marketing strategy?" This question cannot be answered yes or no – the interview must explain the answer.

So, what makes for good questions that you can ask? As mentioned, you could use generic questions that could be used in any interview. These questions should relate to how the company is managed, how decisions are made, how strategy is deployed, what the company's culture is like, and expectations for the position. BY THE WAY, these are not puffery questions or questions to demonstrate that you are a good candidate because you can ask thought-provoking questions (although that is exactly what you are doing), but if you are going to work for this company, these are questions you should want to know the answers to so you can evaluate if this is an organization that you really want to work for. Here are some sample questions you can use, but I urge you to make up a few of your own – after all, you are not the only person reading this guide.

"When you hire me for this position, what are the problems that you want me to tackle first?"

"Assuming I get the job, how are you going to evaluate my job performance in the first six months?"

"Could you describe for me the company's culture?"

"When important changes are being made in your organization, how typically are those changes made?"

"How are significant decisions made in your organization?"

"What role will my position play in developing systems and processes for this division?"

"Can you describe the morale of the people whom I will be working with?"

"Could you please describe your management style?"

"If I were to talk to one of your staff, what would that person tell me about you?" (This question may be a little aggressive, but it is up to you to choose questions you are comfortable asking).

"What are the greatest challenges currently facing your company and/or your department?"

"Why do you enjoy working here?"

"Could you share a bit about how you made it to your current position?"

The second type of questions are more company-specific. These are the types of questions that might be created by reading the company's website, reviewing press releases, or just reading about markets in general. I just did a Google search on "Five Guys Burgers News." Let's say you were going for an interview for a marketing position at Five Guys Burgers. Here are some questions I developed based on reading a few news stories on the company.

"A recent poll suggests Five Guys Burgers is the best burger chain in the country. Why do you think that is?"

"You now have about 1,500 burger stores. How do you maintain consistency of product quality across such a large base of stores?"

"I read an article that says Five Guys Burgers does not use traditional marketing. How do you get customers?"

"I read about Five Guys Burger stores closing in Nevada and California. Why are these stores closing?"

"I read in an article that one of your stores served bad meat and meat that fell on the floor. How do you combat negative publicity when anyone can write just about anything on the Internet?"

What will these questions do for you? Two things. First, in answering these questions, you may get more of an inkling about the person you may be working for, if offered the job. If the interviewer is curt, condescending, or gives you lip service, you may want to consider if you really want to work for the jerk. (Note that a colleague of mine told me I should not use the word "jerk" but rather use the phrase "this type of person." I am sorry, but if you have an interviewer like that, the person is, in my opinion, a "jerk.") He may be exactly that way when you have business problems you want to discuss. On the other hand, if the person gives you thoughtful and articulate answers, that may be an indication that he is a mentor and teacher, and those are the best bosses.

Regardless of how the interviewer answers the questions, you will have demonstrated that you have done some research on the company before coming in for the interview, and knowing something about the company ALWAYS gets you points over those candidates who have not done their research, and who don't know much about the company.

It is also important to understand the chain of command in an organization. Often you will be interviewed by a manager who must get her boss to sign off on you being hired. The boss most likely does not really want to get into too much depth with you. She is leaving that to her manager. In this case, you may only have the opportunity for a quick impression. It is still a good idea to try to develop rapport, but you may want to be briefer and more deferential while remaining poised and confident. One good idea is to state how you appreciate the opportunity for the interview and that you very much admire the company.

WHAT DO YOU KNOW ABOUT OUR COMPANY?

E ven if you've done some research, inevitably you will get asked the question, "What do you know about our company?" Typically, this question is asked because the interviewer wants to tell you about the company and perhaps the position that is currently open. Asking you if you know anything about the company is simply a polite lead-in for the interviewer to start telling you about the company.

So how do you answer this question? Be prepared. How should you be prepared? Simple. Before you go for the interview, go to the company's website. Print off eight to ten pages from the company's website or press releases the company has issued. Then, take the brightest highlighter you can find and highlight several sentences on each page (enough so the highlights can be easily seen). Staple the pages together and put them in a file folder.

Now, when you are asked, "What do you know about our company?" you open up the folder (in a way in which the interviewer can clearly see what is in the folder) then you flip through the pages you printed out, making a point of doing it in a way that the interviewer can clearly see the pages with your highlights on them. As you do so, you say, "Well, I was able to learn a lot about the company from your website and these press releases, but I'd really like to hear you talk about the company from your perspective. I'd particularly like to know more about the company's culture and strategy and why you like working here."

Now you've done two things that will get you credit. First, the interviewer will see that you did some research. Most other candidates will never bother to review the website, never mind printing out pages and highlighting them. Second, you will get points for asking the interviewer to talk about the company, but you've also asked some questions about information THAT you may not find on the website, such as culture, strategy, and why the company is a good place to work. Some companies do include mission statements, visions, and values on their websites, and if they do, make sure you read this information.

The interviewer is going to tell you about the company anyway, you might as well score some points while he or she is doing it. You can also score some extra points if, in addition to researching the company, you've done a little bit of research on the company's competitors. Asking questions about competitors (and naming them) is a great way to demonstrate you've taken your research seriously.

As a final point in this section, be enthusiastic about the company's business. Saying things like, "I wished I'd know about your company before. When I worked at ABC Corp, we really could have used your services." Show a sincere interest in what the company does to generate revenues and serve its customers.

THE SMALLEST PENCIL

As a supervisor and a professor, I like employees and students who take notes. There is an old saying that the shortest pencil is better than the longest memory. You should always have a note pad, and you should take copious notes during the interview. Why? Because you may jot down something that makes for a good follow up question, but many important interviewers (like me) give favorable points to people who take notes. Taking notes just gives the impression that the candidate is serious, and I can project that forward to what the candidate may do during training sessions when he or she is learning the job. My experience is people who take notes during training sessions learn faster and make fewer mistakes than those who don't bother to take notes. So, make sure you have a pad of paper, a pen, and that during the interview, you are scribbling notes down on that pad of paper. Even if you have terrible handwriting, and you hate taking notes, and you have the best memory on the planet, write something on the pad during the interview. Most candidates will not, and you will get points for having done something that reflects well on your organizational abilities and learning style.

DEMONSTRATIONS

S omething you need to develop before you go to an interview is what I call demonstrations. Demonstrations are
nothing more than stories that support all your excellent
traits, characteristics, and experiences. These demonstrations
are designed to show you in the best light possible. Some people
call these demonstrations success stories, illustrations, or examples. They are all designed to do the same thing – demonstration that you have the behavioral characteristics the employer is
looking for. It's not enough to just develop these demonstrations
– you need to write them down and internalize them.

Many professional recruiters and people working in the
human resources department use the same or very similar questions. Therefore, once you have developed a series of demonstrations to answer these questions, you have pretty much covered
most of the questions that you will be asked. I am going to go
over these most common questions in more detail later, but just
to summarize you will get questions that are designed to:

- Allow you to get acquainted with the interviewer
- To measure your interest in the job
- To find out about your experience and your accom-

plishments
- To find out your desires for the future
- Questions that challenge you (what are your weak-
nesses)
- Questions that ask what you would do in certain hypo-
thetical situations
- Questions that show how you behave with others
- Illegal and inappropriate questions
- Questions about salary.

Yes, I know that this is a long list of questions. It is ten questions, and in my experience, about ten questions are what you
can expect to get from an interviewer. Nevertheless, if you are
going to be successful in beating out other candidates, you need
to have answers to all these questions. If you Google "Ten most
common interview questions," you will find numerous websites
that list common interview questions and give recommended
answers. I am not going to include all of that information in
this guide because it is readily available on the Internet; however
I highly recommend that you do additional research over and
above this text to identify those most common questions and to
make sure you have good answers for them all.

A good demonstration includes a description of the task,
some statistics that allow for a quantitative assessment of the
task, and hopefully some achievement that you accomplished
doing that task. A lot of job seekers struggle with creating these
demonstrations, but when you have developed and internalized
them, your interview skills will improve substantially. By the
way, some of these demonstrations may be good to include on
your resume or cover letter.

Many interview websites and coaches recommend using the
STAR method when formulating your demonstrations. STAR is an
acronym for:

Situation: Set the scene and give the necessary details of
your example.

Task: Describe what your responsibility was in that situation.

Action: Explain exactly what steps you took to address it.

Result: Share what outcomes your actions achieved.

So, let's look at an example. Some years ago, I was helping a student who was looking for a job. Doing a mock interview with him, I asked, "Tell me about your most recent job." Expect questions like this – interviewers also know how to ask open-ended questions. My student responded with a brief description of how in order to put himself through university, he worked as a valet parking cars. He indicated to me that he didn't think anyone would be impressed with someone who parks cars for a living. I spent a little time talking about his job and found out that he worked as the valet at a posh restaurant in Beverly Hills. Some nights he parked as many as 200 cars. Because of the location, he parked many very expensive cars, including Bentleys, Maseratis, and Lamborghinis. I also asked him how many cars he had damaged. He said none. So, we changed the way he described his job to the following: "I work as a valet to the stars parking cars at one of the top restaurants in Beverly Hills. On any given night, I will part 200 plus cars, including Bentleys, Maseratis, and Lamborghinis. I am proud to say in over two years, I have never once damaged a single car. I even had one celebrity who insisted that I was the only valet who could park his car."

Now you can see how the new description of his job says so much more about him. Note that because of the added details about the number of cars, types of cars, and location, we have a much greater understanding of this person's capabilities. Also, we read into this description (consciously or subconsciously) certain things about this person's character. To me, I see that he can be trusted (he is parking very expensive cars). I see that he must have some people skills (let's face it, some rich people can be demanding and rude). I see that he is capable (parked thousands of cars with no accidents). I see that he can work under pressure (the valet's at busy restaurants can have lines of demanding customers wanting their cars).

A good demonstration gives us insights into your character. Some people use the word "trait," but it is the same thing. We are really talking about is character traits. And remember, that character is extremely important. Character is more important than skills. As has been said many times, I can teach someone how to use a software program, I cannot teach someone how to get along with other employees in the office. You want your demonstrations to show that you are a person of good character and that you have great character traits. Once again, interviews are in part to determine your personality and personality fit within the organization. You are also trying to find out if the company is a fit for your personality.

As you are developing demonstrations, look at some job ads. Many job ads are looking for the same thing. Here is a list of attributes that you will find on many job ads:

- Works well under pressure
- Gets along well with coworkers
- Good communicator
- Good at solving problems
- Can work in a fast-paced environment
- Fast learner
- Self-starter

- Can work independently
- Has attention to detail
- Good at solving problems.

There are probably a few more, but if you take some time to look at ten or twenty job ads, you will see a common theme. Employers are looking for the same character traits in their employees. Note that I say character traits. Why? Because if you really look at the list above you will see that none of these are skills. I can never teach someone who is not a self-starter, to be a self-starter. I can never teach someone who does not get along well with people to get along well with people. I often wonder why employers bother putting these items in their job ads, because I doubt anyone reading the ad would say, "Oh, I am a terrible communicator, so I won't bother applying for the job." Most people would rate themselves as having all these traits.

Where you can gain an advantage over other candidates is to have ready your demonstrations or stories that prove you have these traits. A good interviewer is going to ask you, "We need someone who is really a good communicator. How are your communication skills?" "Great!" is not an acceptable answer to this question. You need a story or a demonstration. As an example, you might answer, "Well, part of my job as a customer service rep at Wells Fargo was to explain to new customers how saving money in an IRA account works. I am proud to say that I opened more IRA accounts than any other customer service rep at my branch."

Your job now is to get busy and to prepare demonstrations that speak to the most commonly sought character traits by employers. You should have demonstrations that answer each one of the most commonly asked questions. I am not going to go over every possible question, but I will discuss what I see as the most important questions, and how you should answer those questions (using the demonstrations you have developed in advance).

PORTFOLIO

We've talked about printing out information from the company's website, but to be well prepared, there are other documents you should consider bringing along. I recommend that you bring along a couple of copies of your resume. Also, bring along a separate sheet of paper with your references listed. Don't volunteer the reference list unless the interviewer asks for it, but having it ready just shows you are more prepared than the candidate who says she will email the information on references later.

Depending upon the job you are applying for, it may also be a good idea to bring along samples of work that you have performed. I think back over my many years in business and many of the great projects I worked on from annual reports for public companies, to white papers, to articles, to handbooks for employees. I never kept most of these documents, but about fifteen years ago (thanks in part to computers), I started keeping everything. While I am no longer looking for a "job," I still go on interviews because I still do consulting work. I often take along a couple of samples of things I have produced for other client companies. Of course, I hide the names for confidentiality purposes, but being able to hand a sample of your work product to a potential employer will definitely put you ahead of the other candidates, because in my experience, 99% of all candidates will not bring a sample of their work.

Something else you can add to your portfolio is written descriptions of major projects or accomplishments. We've already talked about your demonstrations or stories, but those demonstrations are designed to be quick anecdotes. They are stories you use in response to questions, and most likely should not take you more than a minute or two to relate. How can you showcase a major accomplishment that takes more time to explain? Write it down and hand a copy to the interviewer. I had one project I worked on for about a year and a half that involved redoing accounting records, building a new accounting team, installing a new accounting system, developing accounting policies and procedures, producing financial statements in compliance with generally accepted accounting principles and getting the financials reviewed by a major accounting firm. The result - the owners were able to sell 50% of the company to a private equity firm for $28 million. But that story is too long to use as a demonstration, so I have a one-page description of this project that I leave with potential clients. Think about what you have accomplished, and it may be that you have engaged in projects and activities of broad scope that could be part of your portfolio.

TELL ME ABOUT YOURSELF

Most interviews start off with this seemingly innocuous question, "Tell me about yourself." You might think why the interviewer would ask this question, when the interviewer has your resume sitting right in front of him. Interviewers ask this question to get a sense of your communication skills. Interviewers also use this question to find out more about your personality. How good are you at explaining who you are and what you do? Do you provide too much information, do you speak clearly, do you provide too little information, is your response organized, do you seem like an interesting and likable person. The interviewer is assessing you, and because this is often the first question, it is one of the most important. If you do a bad job of answering this question, the interviewer may tune out and may decide right at this point you are not a suitable candidate.

If you go online and Google "How do I answer the question, tell me about yourself," you will find dozens of websites that can give you a good idea of what to say. I encourage you to review a few of those websites. And because there is so much already on the Internet about this question, I am only going to give you a few simple guidelines here.

- **Don't ramble.** That is what people do who do not prepare in advance. Your answer needs to be organized and rehearsed.
- **Don't just repeat your resume.** Presumably, the interviewer has your resume, so you don't need to cover everything that is on it.
- **Don't include too much detail.** The interviewer doesn't need to know that you were born in Fairview Valley Hospital and lived the first six years of your life in Dearborn, Michigan.
- **Do mention how your experience and abilities make you suitable for this job.** You have the job ad. Most job ads stress three or four skills or character traits the company is looking for. Speak to the job ad using some of the demonstrations I discussed previously.
- **Keep it short.** Your answer to this question should not be longer than two or three minutes.

- **Mention something personal.** Some experts might tell you to keep your answer strictly business. I like to know that someone coming to work for me also has a life outside of work. Sometimes what people do outside of works shows a lot about their character. For instance, mentioning that you run marathons speaks of perseverance and dedication. Mentioning that you help save stray dogs shows you have compassion. However, don't talk about any bad or negative things that might be happening in your life. Nobody wants to hear them, and they may be signs that you will be tied up with your personal issues and not focused on performing at work.

It is important that you write out your answer to this question, review and rewrite it until it is as good as you can make it, and then practice, practice, practice until you have internalized it.

ARE YOU A ZEBRA?

What do zebras have to do with getting a job? Nothing and everything. Ever wonder why we ride horses and not zebras? The reason is that zebras do not get along well with people. Zebras don't even get along that well with other zebras.

At some point in the interview (and maybe at more than one point), the interviewer is going to try to find out if you are a zebra. Do you get along well with people? Typically, the question will be of the form, "Tell me about a time when you had a problem with....a customer, a co-worker, a boss, a subordinate." The interviewer may add, "And how did you solve the problem?" Inexperienced job hunters will rack their brains trying to find an answer to this question, often relating stories of fighting with coworkers or bosses.

The answer to this question is simple. You should never initially admit that you have had a problem with anyone you have worked with. Even better, have a couple of demonstrations ready to show how well you get along with the people you work with. Here are a few examples.

"I can't ever remember having a problem with any of my

bosses. In fact, my last boss and I were very close, and once a month we'd go to dinner with our wives."

"I can't recall having any problems with my coworkers. Louise worked with me at ABC company, and she is the Godmother of my daughter, and Ruby worked with me at XYZ Company, and our families go camping together every Memorial Day Weekend."

"I've always gotten along well with customers. One of my customers actually invited me to her wedding!"

Remember, I said you should never initially admit that you have had a problem with anyone you have worked with. If you answer the question using your positive "get along with people" demonstrations, the interviewer may pass and go on to her next question. However, experienced interviewers may press you. They could say something like, "Come on. Everyone has had a problem with their boss, co-worker, customer, or subordinate at some point in time."

Now you must answer. So be prepared. This is where you need a good demonstration. If you must talk about a situation where you had a problem or disagreement, make sure the disagreement arose out of some moral or ethical judgment relating to other people. What do I mean? The disagreement should not be about you, your salary, your working conditions, your relationships with other employees, your treatment at work and should never be around personality issues. All of these could be signs that you are a zebra.

So how should you answer the question? **You need to find an instance where your disagreement was over making a decision that affected other people, that had legal implications or that had moral and ethical implications.** Here are a few examples.

"Gee, I always got along really well with my boss, but if I have to think about an instance where we had a problem, it was with this customer. Our product has a 90-day warranty. A customer returned one of our machines 92 days after purchase because the machine had stopped working. Technically the product was out of warranty. My boss denied the warranty claim. However, one of our technicians told me clearly that our product was defective. I went to my boss and argued that we should cover the repair costs. We argued back and forth, and I was finally able to convince my boss we should take care of the customer. The customer was elated, and later he purchased three more machines from us."

This story is very effective because the person who is being treated poorly is a customer and not you, so there is no way that the interviewer can infer that you are a problem employee. Second, it shows something about your character – you are willing to do the right thing. Let's look at one more example.

"Sarah and I were put in charge of organizing the company Christmas party. Sarah wanted the party to be employees only, but I wanted the party to include significant others. Sarah was convinced that significant others would ruin the comradery and that we would have more fun with just employees. I always go to my husband's Christmas party, and most companies I worked for also have invited significant others. Sarah and I were at an impasse when I came up with an idea – two parties. I proposed to the manager of our division that we have a late afternoon cocktail and appetizer event at the office, just for employees. Then we would also have a Saturday evening dinner with significant others. The boss agreed, and Sarah and I were able to hold both events for the budget originally set for just one event."

This story is very effective because the person (people) affected are not you, but other employees and significant others. Also, it shows creativity on your part for coming up with a compromise idea that benefited everyone in the company. Let's look at one more example.

"Typically, my boss and I got along very well, but there was one situation that did cause a problem between us. My boss took a business trip to New York. On this trip, he took his wife with him. I am friends with his wife, and when they returned, she was telling me about seeing Lion King on Broadway with my boss's two sisters and their husbands, all who live in New York. When we were processing his expense report, I noted he had expensed six tickets to Lion King at $277.00 for each ticket. Then there was dinner at Gallagher's Steak House for $1,200.00. The company is publicly traded, and this seemed to me like cheating our shareholders. I spoke to my boss about this and pointed out I didn't think it was appropriate. He argued that he worked hard for the company and deserved a little bonus from time to time. I suggested that if he could get the divisional manager to approve it, I would pay it. He came back to me the next day with the divisional manager's approval for two show tickets and only $400 for dinner. "

This story is very effective because the people affected (the shareholders) are not you. Also, it shows that you are looking out for the company and not willing to let other employees steal from the company.

Again, and I am going to put it in capitals NEVER ADMIT THAT YOU HAD A SERIOUS PROBLEM OR ISSUE WITH ANOTHER PERSON YOU WORKED WITH. YOU DON'T WANT TO BE A ZEBRA.

STRENGTHS

One of the most common interview questions has to do with strengths. The question could be phrased in different ways. Here are a few examples:

"What are your greatest strengths?"

"Name three things you do well?"

"What makes you think you are suited for this job?"

All these questions are designed to get you to talk about what you think you are good at. There are three rules in answering these types of questions.

Rule #1: Your strengths should relate to the job. So, if the job is looking for someone with attention to detail, then attention to detail should be one of your strengths. Go back and look at the job ad, so you know what the company is looking for in a successful candidate. (Sidebar: Many candidates fail to read the job ads. Before the interview, read the job ad and highlight the important things that the employer is looking for.)

Rule #2: You should have a demonstration to demonstrate your strength. So, if attention to detail was your strength, you need to talk about something you did that required great attention to detail (and at which you hopefully achieved success).

Rule #3: Your strengths should all be character traits unless the job requires some very specific and unique skills. Remember, an employer can teach skills, but not character traits.

WEAKNESSES

In addition to asking about strengths, an interviewer will most likely ask about weaknesses. Again, like the strengths question, the actual question may be worded differently. Here are some examples:

"Tell me about your greatest weaknesses?"

"Name three things you could improve on?"

"Where do you think you would find this job challenging?"

All these questions are designed to get you to tell the interviewer about where you have problems and issues. So how do you answer this question? You start off by denying that you have any weaknesses, specifically as it relates to the job. Remember, you have a copy of the job ad. When asked this question, take the copy of the job ad out of the folder on your lap, quickly read through the ad, and then respond something like this:

"Well, your ad says you are looking for someone who can work independently, someone who is detail oriented, and someone who is a good communicator. The person you are looking for is me. I don't see that I have any weaknesses that would keep me from doing an excellent job for you."

Now, some interviewers may give you a pass, and move on to the next question. However, experienced interviewers may press you by saying something like, "Oh come on. Everyone has a weakness or needs to improve on something."

Personally, I like to answer this question with a joke, but not everyone is comfortable doing so. You must make sure your response fits your style. But if you use a joke, you could say something like, "Well, my wife thinks I'm not doing a good job in taking out the garbage, so I guess I could improve on that." Even if you come back with a joke, once you get a laugh (assuming the interviewer has a sense of humor), you will need to talk about weaknesses. You have no choice. You must answer.

When you do answer, there are three rules for weaknesses:

Rule #1: Just because you have a weakness does not mean you have to admit it. When you buy a car, the car salesman doesn't tell you that General Motors had 30 products recalled last year. He tells you that the car is great and you're getting a great price. Regardless of how you feel about yourself, don't go on and on about your weaknesses. You have no moral or legal obligation to say anything negative about yourself, and it is your responsibility to say as many positive things about yourself as you can. This rule holds true even if you were fired from your last job for incompetence, and your previous boss told you that you were the worst employee on the planet.

Rule #2: If you are forced to admit to a weakness, make sure it is a weakness of skill, not a character trait. Again, skills can be learned, character traits cannot. So, as an example, you could say something like, "Well, I have to admit I'd like to be better using Excel. I just learned V-Lookup and Pivot Tables, but I really want to learn more."

Rule #3: Once you have admitted one of your skills is lacking, suggest your plan to improve that skill. Following on Rule #2, you could say, "However, I just enrolled in a weekend Advanced Excel course, and I'm really looking forward to putting what I learn to work."

I am going to put this in capitals because it is so important: NEVER ADMIT TO HAVING ANY WEAKNESS OF CHARACTER, ONLY OF SKILLS. And if you admit to a skill weakness, make sure you have a plan of action ready to support your improvement.

GREATEST ACCOMPLISHMENT

One of the questions you will get in an interview at some point or another is a question asking you to describe your greatest accomplishment. For people who are early on in their career, and who maybe don't have much job experience, the tendency may be to think along the lines of personal accomplishments. Personal accomplishments are great, but business accomplishments are even better. Think back over your work career and try and come up with something that made a difference to your employer. If you cannot, then try to come up with something that helped other people. As an example, if you ran a marathon and you helped build a shelter for homeless people, mention the shelter for homeless people. Just be careful to make sure your greatest accomplishment is not something that is risky such as skydiving or flying down a mountain in one of those squirrel suits. Employers don't want employees whose off hours activities might get them killed.

SOMETHING YOU
DID THAT HELPED
THE COMPANY

Depending upon the position, the company may be looking for what I call a grinder. A grinder is a person who sits at her desk, rolls up her proverbial sleeves, and gets busy processing whatever it is she processes. The company is looking for someone who can handle a lot of similar transactions quickly and without error. If that's the type of job you have applied for, then you should have some examples of your ability to process transactions. Think back to what you have done in the past and try to quantify it – did you process 50 or 500 accounts payable invoices in a day? Did you resolve 10 or 100 customer inquiries a day? Being able to put your work production in numerical terms is an asset (both in your oral demonstrations and in your resume).

But in some jobs, the company is looking for less of a grinder and more of a problem solver. With these companies, you will get questions like, "Tell me about a time where you made a change that improved profits or efficiency?" If you get these types of questions, you need to have some answers. Unfortunately, most of us don't record the day to day improvements we make. We only remember the big changes that happen, and if we are a clerk or some other mid to lower level employee, those changes may not be yours to take credit for.

It may take you a while, but if you think about it, you should be able to come up with at least three examples. These examples don't have to be monumental; they just need to show a little improvement in something that was being done less efficiently in the past. Here as some examples from people I have helped prepare for the interview process.

"The people with company credit cards were always losing their receipts. I set up an email address expenses@XYZcorp.com and had the credit card users immediately take a picture of the receipt when they used the credit card then email it off of their phones to that email address. This simple step resolved the issue of missing credit card receipts."

"Our company did a check run every two weeks, and then one of the owners would sit there with 200 checks to hand sign. A lot of the checks were small amounts. I suggested we try to use our company credit cards for small purchases, and it cut down our printed check run from 200 to about 50."

"We kept an electronic copy of every supplier invoice in QuickBooks and another copy in the cloud on OneDrive, then we printed every invoice and filed them in file folders. Given that we already had two electronic copies, I suggest we not bother filing paper copies in a filing cabinet. This saves about four hours a week."

I am sure you get the idea. Think back to what you did at previous employers. Simple changes can often have significant results, and if you can remember two or three, then you can talk about it. It shows you can be more than just a grinder, but you can help contribute to efficiency and profitability.

WHY DID YOU OR ARE YOU LEAVING YOUR PREVIOUS EMPLOYER?

Interviewers ask this question to try to find out if you were fired, or if you left or are leaving your job because you are a zebra (see the chapter on Zebras). The rule here is simple. If your last job was working for the worst company, with the worst boss, and the worst group of coworkers on the planet, and you hated every minute of it, and the company was crooked, and the CEO went to jail, you are not going to mention one word of any of that to the interviewer. You are going to tell the interviewer that you are looking for the opportunity to take on more responsibilities, to put more of your talents and abilities to work, and to find an environment where you can make a meaningful contribution to the success of the business. Never, ever, ever speak disparagingly about a coworker, a subordinate, a supervisor, or a previous company. If you had a bad experience, evade the question and talk about the opportunity you are looking for in the future. If pressed (which some interviewers will do), find something great to say about your former employer (even bad employers have some redeeming factors even if you must dig deep to find them).

If you were or are a student, it is also acceptable to say you left an employer so you could focus on your studies and completing a degree more in line with your career goals.

YOUR RESUME

This guide is all about the interview. So, why am I bringing up your resume? It's not to teach you how to prepare a resume (although I do have my opinions about what should and should not be included). If you want to know how to prepare a resume, just Google and there are hundreds of websites that will give you tips on how to recreate your resume, and resume dos and don'ts. Take the time to review at least four or five of these sites to get some ideas on how to make your own resume more impressive.

The reason I bring up resumes is because whatever you do put on a resume could lead to a question. Savvy interviewers will try to catch you in having embellished your resume by adding descriptions of tasks performed that you actually have not performed, detailing responsibilities and accomplishments that you did not have, and listing software systems and office tools that you really don't know how to use. If it's on your resume, you need to be able to explain it in a way that the interviewer is convinced that you really know what you are doing. I am going to give you some examples that I have taken from resumes that have been submitted to some of my client companies for positions those companies had open.

Resume claimed: "Supervised and managed four employees."

A good interviewer would ask, "What was your process for managing these employees?" If you assigned work, evaluated job performance, issued warnings, did annual reviews, and recommended increases in compensation, then you really did manage and supervise four employees. However, I have asked this question to candidates who did none of the above, and therefore could not explain what they managed. Really, they were not supervisors.

Resume claimed: "Managed accounts receivable."

A good interviewer would ask, "How did you manage accounts receivable?" If you set credit policies, approved credit terms, worked collections, approved write-offs and write-downs, drafted collection letters, and supervised accounts receivable staff, then you really did manager accounts receivable. But if all you did was send out invoices and post payments, you are performing the work of clerk, and not managing anything.

A recruiter friend of mine interviewed a candidate who claimed on his resume to have SEO experience. When asked to explain how he had used his SEO skills to improve the rankings of his employer's website, he finally admitted he had not really done any SEO work but had watched a YouTube video about it.

Your resume could be the source for many of the questions you do get asked during your interview, so be prepared. Here is what you should do:

1) Review everything you have listed on your resume as a responsibility, accomplishment, experience, and/or skill and be prepared to describe in detail exactly what work you performed.

2) Get rid of any fuzzy statements that are difficult to explain, such as (found on a real resume) "Responded to customer concerns with speed and accuracy." If you

were asked to explain your process or system for doing so, that would be a very difficult question to answer.

3) Make sure you do not embellish your resume by claiming to have experience or knowledge of activities you are only peripherally familiar with (in other words, no lying on your resume – ever).

INAPPROPRIATE
QUESTIONS

By law, there are questions that an interviewer cannot ask you. Employers cannot ask you about the following information:

- Age
- Race, ethnicity, or color
- Gender or sex
- Country of national origin or birthplace
- Religion
- Disability
- Marital or family status or pregnancy.

Will you ever get asked these kinds of questions? Yes, you may, for two reasons. First, sometimes interviewers just slip up. This particularly happens if the person doing the interview is new to it or doesn't interview very often. The other reason is that the interviewer may be testing you. The last thing an employer wants is someone who is going to try to sue the company at the slightest provocation. So how you answer an inappropriate question is very important.

Let's say the interviewer asks, "So, how many children do

you have?" How do you respond?

What you don't want to do is to respond in a way that is threatening, or that might indicate you could cause trouble. So, you wouldn't answer: "Hey, California labor law says you can't ask me that question, and I'm going to report you to the labor board!" You might very well go and report the company, but if you answer this way, you will never get hired.

The first thing you should think about is, do you mind answering the question? If you don't mind, then answer it. If you do mind, then you might say something like, "Is that question really relevant to the job? Typically, most employers don't ask those kinds of questions." If the interviewer forgets the rules, or if the interviewer is just testing you, most likely the interviewer will retract the question and move on. You could also say something like, "As a professional, I always organize my personal life such that it allows me to do my job and does not affect my career responsibilities."

While it is a no-no for the interviewer to ask certain questions, there are no rules against you providing any of this information on a voluntary basis. Remember, you are being judged primarily on your character and the interviewer's perception of how you will perform on the job. Personal information, including some of the information about which an employer cannot ask, could affect the employer's judgment of you as a candidate. Let me make it perfectly clear, there are probably employers who may be prejudiced against people's ethnicity, race, religion, sexual orientation, and so on. However, having worked with well over 100 companies, I have never met such an employer. Every employer I have ever worked with has as his or her priority one thing – can the person do the job.

Employers are always trying to assess the person's suitability for the position. Let's say I am hiring for a position where I want the person to work a lot of overtime. Now, if I know that the candidate has two school age children who must be picked up from daycare by 5 PM every day, I might think the candidate would not be suitable. I can't ask if you have two school age children, so I might try to ask you some other questions to see if you will tell me, like asking about your last vacation. If you tell me it was to Disneyland, then it is a good bet you have children.

You want to demonstrate to your employer that you are the best candidate for the job, so put yourself in the employer's shoes. Think about what concerns you might have, if you were doing the hiring. Then disclose information that the employer is not allowed to ask, to your advantage. Let's carry our example a little further. Let's say you do have two school aged children, and they do have to be picked up by 5 PM. Maybe you have things structured, so that is not a problem. When the employer asks, "Can you work a lot of overtime?" What he really wants to ask is if you have kids who are going to be a problem. You volunteer even before being asked by saying something like this: "It sounds to me that you're going to need someone to work a lot of overtime to get caught up and to get the department in order. That's not a problem with me. My husband always picks up my two daughters after school because he always gets off at 4 PM, and if ever he is busy, my sister lives around the corner from me, and her son goes to the same school."

Now you have given the employer information he wanted to know but could not ask, and you have even strengthened your chances of getting the job in a couple of ways, depending upon the job. On the one hand, you have shown that your children will not be a problem with you working overtime. On the other hand, you have divulged something that makes you more stable – a mother with children is less likely to quit her job for a couple of hundred dollars a month, or to quit her job to move to Texas to be close to the new boyfriend.

Alternatively, you could provide some other evidence that you are reliable, such as mentioning that you consistently worked overtime at a previous job, or that you came in on weekends to make sure the department did not get behind. Again, use your discretion, share what you are comfortable in sharing and have your demonstrations ready to show that you are a candidate of worthwhile character.

So, when you are in an interview, think about what might be important from the employer's perspective and disclose that information if you think doing so will give you some advantage or that you will be looked upon more favorably than other candidates.

Let's look at one more example. Today in most government institutions and many private companies, there are goals to increase diversity. What does that mean? Typically, it means hiring anyone who is not a male white Caucasian of European descent to achieve stated diversity objectives. It could be to your advantage in getting hired if you can identify with a minority ethnicity. One of my colleagues didn't think I should include this discussion in my guidebook. But I disagree. We live in a society where other people make the rules. It is up to each of us to take advantage of the rules if it is to our advantage to do so. Further, I would say we have an obligation to take advantage of every opportunity that favors us. I don't necessarily agree with every tax deduction written into the tax code, but if those deductions save me taxes, I am going to take them.

Today we have a lot of mixed couples, and therefore we have mixed children. My own children are of mixed race. An employer is allowed to note physical characteristics about you but cannot ask about your race or ethnicity. Your race and/or ethnicity may not be obvious. You could get passed over if the employer thinks you are a white Caucasian in favor of a Hispanic, Asian, or Black. Therefore, it could be to your advantage to mention your race and/or ethnicity. Of course, you would want to do it in a way that is not too obvious. Let's say your mother is of Mexican heritage, and she married a man of British heritage whose last name was Thompson, and your name is David. It may not be obvious that you qualify as Hispanic. Try to find a way to bring it into the conversation when you are talking about something else, like travel, foods you like, or personal pastimes. Maybe mention that on your last vacation, you visited your grandmother in Mexico City.

All that being said, you need to be discrete in sharing personal information. Some candidates just share way too much information. And unless that information can play a role in getting you a job, leave it out. How do you know? Think about it. Put yourself in the employer's shoes. Think about the places you've worked at previously. What would you like to know about someone before hiring that person? A recruiter friend tells me sometimes candidates share information that makes him uncomfortable. Watch the personal information you share, and make sure it is being shared for the right reasons.

HOW MUCH DO YOU WANT TO EARN?

Most interviewers will ask you how much you want to make. The general rule is to avoid all conversations about compensation during the interview. Wait until the company has made a formal job offer before you ask about pay, vacation time, benefits, bonuses, and so on. However, some interviewers may press you. If so, you need to be prepared. Fortunately, thanks to the Internet, you can find out how much just about any job pays. I just Googled "Accounts Payable Clerk Salary," and the following result showed:

"The average Accounts Payable Clerk salary in Los Angeles, CA, is $47,636 as of June 27, 2019, but the range typically falls between $42,961 and $53,313."

Let's say you are applying for an Accounts Payable job, and the interviewer asks about compensation. Open the folder sitting on your lap, pull out the printout from your Google search and say something like: "Salary.com says that the average pay for an accounts payable clerk in Los Angeles is around $48,000 per year. I would expect a company like yours who is looking for top talent would most likely pay something more than the average, and of course, I'd be happy with that."

Then, change the topic. Again, you don't want to spend time in the interview talking about compensation, so move on and ask more of your questions.

BODY LANGUAGE

I debated with myself if I should put the topic of body language at the beginning or at the end. Why? Because body language is an extremely important part of how you are perceived by other people. Our subconscious evaluates every person we meet based on preconceived stereotypes developed over our lifetime of dealing with people and based on our cultural perspectives. I believe some of that has even been hardwired into our genes and part of the knowledge base that has been passed on from generation to generation. The impact of body language is so great that it can make or break the interview, and sometimes it does so on an entirely subconscious level.

I remember interviewing candidates for a controller job, and we had two candidates that had very similar qualifications. Either candidate, based on their education and experience, could have done the job. I had both candidates interview with four people from the company, including me. After the interviews, I sat in the conference room with the other interviewers with the resumes for both candidates on the table. I asked, "Who do we hire?" Our discussion focused mostly on experience, education, and if the candidates would fit into the company culture. Then one of the interviewers said, "I can't explain why, but there is something about candidate X that just makes me uncomfortable. I am not sure what it is, but I don't think we should hire him." And we didn't.

Why do I tell this story? Because that was an example of the subconscious evaluation of this candidate most likely based upon that person's body language. In other words, it's a gut feel or intuition. Is that fair? Maybe not. Does that happen? Absolutely. I think body language is important enough that you should probably find a book on it and read the entire book. However, for those of you who aren't prepared to do that, I will give you a few body language tips here that will increase the likelihood of you being perceived in a favorable light by the interviewer.

Smile – It sounds simple, but some people just have natural smiles, and everyone knows someone whose smile can light up a room. For many of us, smiling does not come naturally. Get in front of the mirror and practice. Smiling makes a huge difference in how you are perceived.

Sit Up – Don't slouch in your chair. Sit up with your back against the back of your chair with your feet on the ground.

Eye Contact – When you are answering questions, make eye contact. You don't want to stare at the interviewer, but I have been in interviews where after asking a question, the candidate answers by looking at the ceiling or even worse, looking at the floor. Body language experts suggest that people who look at the floor when answering a question are lying. If you are in a group interview, make sure you make eye contact with everyone, don't just focus on the one person who may have asked a question.

Use Hand Gestures – Ever watch great speakers? One thing you will notice is that their hands are active. Their hands work to help communicate their stories. Get into the habit of using your hands to help you tell your stories.

Acknowledge What Others Are Saying – When you are listening to the interviewer, use your body to show that you are hearing and understanding what you are being told. That typically can be in the form of nodding your head and using facial expressions to show your interest, amazement, or dismay. It could also be certain hand gestures used in reaction to what you hear.

Mirror the Interviewer – Try to sit and speak like the interviewer. If the interviewer clasps his hands together on the desk, do the same (obviously without being too obvious). If the interview leans forward across the table, do the same. If the interview speaks softly or loudly, do the same.

Avoid Restless Behavior – Ever notice that some people tap their feet, twist their hair, pick at a favorite mole, or move their leg up and down? Many of us have subconscious restless behaviors that we engage in. If that's you, make your best efforts to keep these behaviors under control during an interview.

Handshake – We make significant judgments based on someone's handshake. Most of us don't want to shake hands with a jelly fish, and we don't want to shake hands with a bone crusher. Your handshake should be firm, not too strong, and not too weak. Shake hands with a friend and ask for tips on how you could make it better. Make eye contact during your handshake, and of course, smile. If you suffer from sweaty palms, carry a cloth with you and wipe your hand just before the shake.

ENDING THE INTERVIEW AND FOLLOW UP

A s the interview comes to an end, it is important that you find out what the process is for hiring, and the timeline. You need to know when the company plans to make a decision, will you need to interview with anyone else, are references needed (which you should have ready – don't say you'll email them later), what the decision making process is and the anticipated starting date. Having this information allows you to follow up effectively after the interview. If the interviewer says that the company expects to narrow the field of candidates down to three by the end of next week, then by the end of next week, you should be following up to see if your name is on the list. Following up is extremely important because even if you are not one of the final three, it may be that by the time the company has narrowed it down to the final three, one or more of those candidates may be off the market. By that time, the interviews will be a fuzzy memory for the interviewer, but if you have stayed in contact (without being a pest), there is an excellent chance you will be picked to fill the vacant spot.

Finally, after the interview is completed, you need to send a thank you note. Today it is acceptable to do so by email. I am presuming you were smart enough to get the email of the interviewer. Make sure you do. Your thank you email should: 1) thank the interviewer for his/her time, 2) express pleasure at meeting the interviewer, 3) reconfirm your interest in the position, 4) express your commitment to solving the problems the company and/or position is facing and 5) reconnect to the interviewer on a personal level. A simple "thank you" is not enough. There are many good examples of sample thank you letters available on the Internet. Below is an example of a well-crafted thank you email.

Dear Mr. Garcia:

"Thank you very much for meeting with me on Friday to discuss the accounts payable position. I really enjoyed meeting with you, and I am glad to know that you are a fellow Lakers Fan. Perhaps I will see your courtside at one of the games.

I am very excited at the opportunity of joining your team at ABC Company. The backlog situation in the accounts payable department sounds challenging. I am ready to roll up my sleeves and get that backlog fixed.

I look forward to hearing from you soon about the position and further to our discussions, if I don't hear from you by April 10, I will reach out to you.

Thanks again.

Your Name.

CONCLUSION

Hopefully, you will follow my guidelines. If you do, you will be miles ahead of the other candidates, who have not read this information and/or not acted on the information they have read. To get hired, you don't have to be perfect, you just need to show the company that you are a little better than the next candidate, and by using my techniques, you will be. Remember, it is not just about getting a job. It is about getting the best job. The job you want, the job that pays the most, and the job that will best further your career.

I have tried to create a guide that is a quick read, but that contains information that you can apply right away on your next job interview. However, there are two things you should know. First, interviewing well takes practice. You will do better the more you interview. So, if you are a job seeker, go on as many interviews as you possibly can, even if it's just for the experience. Second, your ability to use your education, earn top dollar, and gain wealth are contingent upon you getting the best jobs. The better you become at interviewing, the greater the likelihood of you landing those better jobs. My guide is not the be all and the end all. Use my guide, put my ideas to work, but keep researching and learning. The more you understand how critical the interview is to your success, the better you will do on interviews.

I'd love to hear your job interview stories. My email address is mmanahan@csudh.edu. Please let me know if any of these techniques helped you land that dream job. And if you come up with any great ideas you think I should put in my next edition, please let me know.

Good luck and happy interviewing.

* * *

FOLLOW MICHAEL MANAHAN ON HIS WEBSITE:

www.bizrap.org

SHARE YOUR INTERVIEW STORY ON:

mmanahan@csudh.edu

BOOKS BY THIS AUTHOR

SECRETS TO RAISING CAPITAL

Secrets to Raising Capital is the definitive guide on how to get funding for your business. Unlike other books on raising capital, it is not a list of lenders, investment bankers and investors nor is it filled with instructions on how to value your business or the difference between angel investors and private equity funds. The content of Secrets to Raising Capital is unique. The challenge faced by the business looking to obtain funding is convincing the money source to actually make the loan or the investment. That's where Secrets to Raising Capital comes in.

This easy to read, strategy filled book is packed full of insights and actionable ideas on what to do, and how to do it, to make sure your business get's the money it needs. This book contains the secrets that money guys won't tell you, and most CFOs and consultants don't know. You'll find information on what never to say to a money guy, how to handle deal killers, and how to deliver a compelling presentation. You'll also find out how you can ruin a potential funding in one sentence. Secrets to Raising Capital is packed with pages of dos, don't, how tos, rules and instructions.

It's not some theoretical book from academia, but a hands-on guide with real life examples. And it's not just for early stage companies and startups. The secrets included in this book will be of value to any CEO or CFO trying to raise capital—even in larger corporations and established companies. It doesn't matter how good you think your business is, or how good a manager you are, there are hundreds of reasons why you may not be getting the funding you need. Understanding the process of raising capital is key to funding your business.

In Secrets to Raising Capital you'll discover how the money world works, and how you can raise money for your business the easiest and fastest way possible.

ABOUT THE AUTHOR

MICHAEL S. MANAHAN

Mr. Manahan is a financial strategist, change expert and educator. During his successful career as a financial executive and consultant, Mr. Manahan has helped companies raise in excess of $250 million. Mr. Manahan has worked with more than 100 management teams, as an external consultant or advisor, and as a member of the management team.  He has held the position of chief financial officer for four companies, including three publicly traded companies and a division of a multi-billion-dollar furniture manufacturer. He has held senior finance positions in several other companies.

Mr. Manahan has more than 30 years of financial, executive, organizational and strategic management experience with a diverse group of companies operating in such sectors as real estate development, industrial distribution, consumer and industrial services, computer software, Internet services, healthcare, food manufacturing, entertainment, energy, furniture manufacturing, Internet retailing, construction and consumer products. Further, Mr. Manahan has assisted companies in structuring and completing joint ventures, acquisitions, divestitures, financings and reorganizations, as well as coaching companies through the pre-IPO stage.

Mr. Manahan has extensive experience in SEC reporting, corporate finance, public markets, investor relations and corporate development. Pursuing a life-long love of educating, Mr. Manahan has held numerous engagements to coach CEOs the effective communication styles and management strategies, and is also a professor in the School of Business and Public Policy at California State University, Dominguez Hills where he teaches accounting and finance to CEOs of the future.

Mr. Manahan is a graduate of the British Columbia Institute of Technology with a major in financial management. In 2005, Mr. Manahan enrolled at Pepperdine University in the doctorate of the organization change program and completed the course work, although he did not complete his doctoral dissertation. Mr. Manahan received his Master of Business Administration from Pepperdine in 1992. Mr. Manahan lives in Long Beach, California and has two wonderful daughters, Genevieve and Kimberly.

ACKNOWLEDGMENT

I thank my colleagues who took the time to review my manuscript, who critiqued and corrected my writing, and who gave me countless ideas and suggestions for improving the end-product. Those colleagues include Professor Dr. Thomas Norman, Professor Dr. Vera Teller, and Human Resource and Recruiting Specialist, Travis Poortinga. I also thank the many people I worked with in my career who contributed to the life experiences that made this book possible.

Made in the USA
Las Vegas, NV
23 January 2024

84800128R00059